Original title:
Love's New Dawn

Copyright © 2024 Swan Charm
All rights reserved.

Author: Johan Kirsipuu
ISBN HARDBACK: 978-9916-89-733-1
ISBN PAPERBACK: 978-9916-89-734-8
ISBN EBOOK: 978-9916-89-735-5

Dawn's Holy Embrace

In the stillness, morning breaks,
A whisper from the heavens calls,
Light unfurls, as darkness shakes,
Embraced by grace, the soul enthralls.

Golden rays on nature's face,
Each leaf aglow, a sacred sign,
In tranquil depths, we find our place,
With each heartbeat, love divine.

The heavens paint with vibrant hues,
A canvas touched by hands of light,
In every shadow, hope renews,
As stars fade softly into night.

The birds sing hymns to greet the morn,
Their melodies lift hearts with cheer,
In dawn's embrace, we are reborn,
Through faith and trust, we quell our fear.

With every breath, let gratitude rise,
In sacred stillness, we unite,
Each moment shared beneath the skies,
In dawn's embrace, we find our light.

Resurrection of Tenderness

In the quiet dawn of grace,
Love awakens from its slumber,
Gentle hands of mercy touch,
Healing wounds we too remember.

From ashes rise the hearts once torn,
With whispers softly born anew,
The tenderness of every thorn,
Bears blossoms kissed by morning dew.

In shadows cast by doubt and fear,
The light of kindness breaks our chains,
Revealing paths where souls can steer,
United, love forever reigns.

Spiritual Symphony of Togetherness

Together we shall sing the song,
Of hope that binds each wandering heart,
In harmony, both brave and strong,
A melody where love takes part.

Each note a breath of sacred truth,
Resonating through the night,
A dance of faith, of ancient youth,
Creating bonds that shine so bright.

In every beat, the pulse of grace,
Connecting us through trials faced,
A symphony in time and space,
Where every soul is interlaced.

The Enlightened Heart's Journey

With every step upon this land,
The heart seeks wisdom, pure and vast,
In every grain and gentle hand,
A truth unfurls, a shadow cast.

Each challenge forms a sacred path,
A lesson written in the stars,
Emerging from the storm's fierce wrath,
We rise, our spirits healed from scars.

The journey leads to sacred space,
Where kindness blooms and shines so bright,
In unity we find our place,
An enlightened heart, our guiding light.

Radiant Echoes of Promise

In echoes soft, the promises ring,
A chorus heard in the stillness deep,
Where dreams take flight on faith's own wing,
And every joy is ours to keep.

With radiant light, the dawn unfolds,
The warmth of love ignites the day,
In stories whispered, hope retold,
A legacy, come what may.

Let every act of faith resound,
A legacy of grace bestowed,
In every heart, a love profound,
To guide us on this chosen road.

Ascending Together into Grace

In the quiet dawn we rise,
Hearts aligned with sacred sighs.
Hands entwined in humble prayer,
We seek the light, His love to share.

Each step we take, a guided way,
Beneath the blue of endless day.
Together we tread the path so bright,
United in faith, we embrace the light.

With spirits soaring, hopes entwined,
In God's embrace, our souls refined.
The grace that flows from heart to heart,
A sacred bond that will not part.

Through trials faced, our faith remains,
In every loss, in every gain.
We rise above with each new dawn,
Together as one, our fears withdrawn.

In this journey, closely knit,
Awareness deepens, we shall not quit.
With love as our guide, we rise and live,
In grace, we find, we learn to give.

Spirit-Led Awakening

Awake, O soul! The day is new,
The Spirit calls, our hearts to renew.
In whispers soft, His presence near,
We find our path, we shed our fear.

With wings of faith, we take to flight,
In the embrace of holy light.
Each moment blooms with grace divine,
In sacred rhythm, hearts align.

Let not the world distract our gaze,
For in His love, we find our ways.
The gentle touch of kindness shared,
Reflects the love that we have bared.

As dawn breaks forth, our spirits soar,
With every heartbeat, we seek for more.
In unity, our voices blend,
A chorus sweet, our souls transcend.

Awake, O heart! Embrace the call,
For in His grace, we find our all.
Together, led by spirit's flame,
We awaken love, rejoice in His name.

The Promised Presence

In the stillness, His voice we hear,
A comfort found, to calm our fear.
The promise given, ever near,
In darkest nights, He draws us clear.

Through every storm, our anchor stands,
In loving arms, He understands.
With gentle mercy, we are blessed,
In trials faced, we find our rest.

Together, we walk this sacred ground,
In whispered prayers, His presence found.
With hope restored, our spirits rise,
In trusting hearts, our truth belies.

Unfailing love that we can know,
In every seed of faith we sow.
The promised light will lead the way,
In every moment, night or day.

In His embrace, we cease to roam,
For in His heart, we find our home.
The promised presence, strong and true,
Forever guides, in all we do.

Celestial Roots of Connection

Beneath the stars, our hearts unite,
In celestial grace, we seek the light.
Roots entwined in sacred soil,
In love's embrace, we find our toil.

With each heartbeat, our spirits sing,
In harmony, His praises ring.
The branches stretch, the leaves unfold,
In every story, faith is told.

Through trials faced, we stand as one,
In shared beliefs, the victory won.
Each connection blooms, a sacred thread,
In love's design, our spirits fed.

As dawn awakens, shadows flee,
Together, we walk in unity.
With every prayer, our souls align,
In the divine, our paths entwine.

Celestial roots that bring us peace,
In each embrace, our worries cease.
Through love we flourish, grow, and stand,
In the grace bestowed, forever hand in hand.

Spiritual Blossoming of Hearts

In silence blooms the heart's true grace,
Awakening love in every place.
The spirit's song, a gentle breeze,
Whispers softly through the trees.

Each petal bright, a glance from above,
Reflects the purity of divine love.
In unity, our souls entwine,
Like vines that climb, our paths divine.

Within this garden, faith does grow,
With every prayer, the light does flow.
Each moment cherished, filled with peace,
In sacred trust, our worries cease.

Let kindness rule, let mercy reign,
Through trials faced, through joy and pain.
With open hearts, we walk this road,
Revealing love, our greatest ode.

Whispers in the Morning Light

In dawn's embrace, the world awakes,
Soft whispers dance in gentle lakes.
The sky adorned in hues of gold,
Speaks of promises yet untold.

Each ray of sun, a guiding hand,
Leads us forth upon this land.
In quiet moments, souls connect,
A tapestry of love we weave and reflect.

The morning's glow, a sacred sign,
Reminds us of the love divine.
With every breath, we find our place,
In the rhythm of His grace.

So let us take this brand new day,
With open hearts, let us not sway.
In union, let our spirits rise,
A chorus lifted to the skies.

Holy Moments of Togetherness

In gathering there, our spirits share,
The holy light in love's warm care.
Each smile exchanged, a sacred thread,
Binding hearts where faith is led.

In laughter's echo, blessings flow,
As hands unite, the love does grow.
In gentle moments, life's embrace,
Reflects the depth of heaven's grace.

With every prayer, our souls ignite,
In sacred bonds, our hearts take flight.
Together, we rise on wings of trust,
In holy love, our spirits gust.

Every whisper tells a tale,
Of faith unshaken when shadows pale.
In unity, our hearts will stand,
In holy moments, hand in hand.

The Radiance of Mutual Devotion

In quiet moments, love does shine,
Reflecting grace as hearts align.
A light so bright, it leads the way,
In mutual hope, we choose to stay.

With steadfast faith, our burdens shared,
In every smile, a heart is bared.
Through trials faced, our spirits blend,
In devotion's glow, we find our friend.

Through storms and calm, we journey forth,
To cherish love of endless worth.
In tender trust, we speak and learn,
From every challenge, we discern.

The path of light, where grace unfolds,
Radiates warmth, a love that holds.
In mutual devotion, souls ignite,
Together we walk towards the light.

The Chorus of Celestial Hearts

In the stillness of the night,
Angels sing with pure delight.
Every star, a gentle gleam,
Whispers truth in sacred dream.

Voices rise in harmony,
A symphony, divinely free.
Every note, a stroke of light,
Guiding souls toward the bright.

Hearts unite in prayerful song,
In this choir, we belong.
Faith ignites, a fire within,
Evermore, we rise and spin.

From the heavens, love descends,
With each heartbeat, mercy blends.
Celestial rhythms guide our feet,
As we dance where spirits meet.

In this chorus, we proclaim,
Forever blessed, we call His name.
With each echo, joy imparts,
The melody of celestial hearts.

New Horizons of Grace

Through valleys low and mountains high,
We seek the light, we lift our eye.
Embracing change, we find our way,
To new horizons, dawn's soft sway.

Each step we take, a path unfolds,
In faith, the heart of love upholds.
With every breath, a chance to grow,
In grace, the seeds of joy we sow.

In unity, we stand as one,
The journey brightens with the sun.
With open hearts, we strive to share,
The precious gift of love and care.

Reviving spirits, hope's embrace,
In every moment, find His grace.
The world transformed, a radiant sight,
In new horizons, endless light.

Together, we shall bravely tread,
Where grace and mercy gently spread.
In every trial, we find our place,
On this journey of sacred grace.

Inspired by Divine Kinship

In every heartbeat, love's refrain,
A bond that binds, a holy chain.
In divine kinship, we find our worth,
Each soul aflame, ignites the earth.

With tender hands, we lift the weak,
In every gesture, kindness speaks.
Through laughter shared and tears that flow,
In sacred ties, our blessings grow.

Remembered souls, both near and far,
Guiding lights, our shining star.
In unity, we find our song,
In divine kinship, we belong.

Each moment shared, a gift of grace,
In every smile, His warm embrace.
Together, woven in His plan,
Divine kinship, hand in hand.

For in our hearts, the truth resides,
A love that grows with every stride.
Inspired by faith, we shall renew,
This kinship blessed, forever true.

Sunlit Conversations of the Soul

In the morning's golden glow,
Silent whispers softly flow.
Conversations rich with grace,
In the spirit's warm embrace.

Every word, a sacred spark,
Illuminates the deepest dark.
With hearts open and minds so clear,
We find communion ever near.

In nature's chorus, souls connect,
Reflecting love and deep respect.
With sunlit rays, our spirits soar,
In conversations, we explore.

Through laughter bright and solemn song,
In the dance of life, we belong.
Each moment shared, a treasure rare,
Sunlit dialogues in the air.

With open eyes, we seek the divine,
In every thought, His light will shine.
In conversations of the soul,
Together, we will seek the whole.

Graceful Unfolding of Souls

In shadows deep, where spirits dwell,
A gentle light begins to swell.
With each new breath, we rise and bend,
In grace, our hearts find paths to mend.

The whispers soft, like morning dew,
Their sacred song speaks pure and true.
In unity, we dance and glide,
In love's embrace, the soul's delight.

From darkness born, the flames ignite,
A tapestry woven in gentle light.
The journey long, yet ever bright,
In grace we stand, a wondrous sight.

As petals fall in autumn's grace,
We find our peace in time and space.
With open hearts, we seek the whole,
In every story, a sacred scroll.

Each tear we shed, a diamond shines,
In trials faced, the spirit climbs.
With every heartbeat, trust we sow,
In love's embrace, our spirits grow.

The Reverent Union

In sacred halls where silence reigns,
Two souls entwined, the love remains.
In whispered prayers, their hopes ascend,
A bond eternal, none can rend.

Through trials fierce and shadows cast,
Their faith unyielding, steadfast.
With hands held firm, and spirits wide,
In unity, they find their guide.

Each moment shared, a sacred gift,
In gentle glances, hearts uplift.
Through storms that bow, they steadfast stand,
In reverence, they trust love's hand.

In laughter sweet, and tears sincere,
In every heartache, love draws near.
Their paths entwined, a sacred rite,
In morning's breath, they find the light.

Under starlit skies, they vow
To journey forth in love's sacred plow.
With every heartbeat, souls align,
In reverent union, they brightly shine.

Seraphic Serenade

With wings of light, the angels sing,
In harmony, the heavens bring.
A melody that stirs the soul,
In seraphic waves, we are made whole.

Upon the winds, their voices soar,
In sacred notes, forevermore.
Each chord a whisper, soft and sweet,
In symphony, our hearts repeat.

The rhythm flows like rivers wide,
In every echo, love's abide.
A tender call that weaves the night,
In every heart, a spark of light.

Through fields of dreams, the spirits glide,
In search of truth with love as guide.
With every note, the world transcends,
In seraphic serenade, love mends.

Under the stars, we find our place,
In gentle arms, a warm embrace.
With every breath, a sacred hymn,
In melody divine, our spirits brim.

Dawn's Gentle Revelation

With whispers soft, the dawn brings light,
A sacred promise, pure and bright.
In every ray, the truth unfolds,
A gentle warmth, the heart beholds.

The sky awakes in shades of gold,
In tender hues, the day unfolds.
Each moment born, a fresh embrace,
In light's soft glow, we find our place.

The world anew, a canvas wide,
Where faith and hope walk side by side.
With open hearts, we greet the morn,
In dawn's sweet light, our spirits are born.

From shadows past, we rise and sing,
In gratitude for what days bring.
With every breath, a prayer we weave,
In dawn's embrace, we dare believe.

In stillness found, the soul's delight,
In gentle revelation, pure and bright.
With every sunrise, we are reborn,
In love's embrace, forever sworn.

Seraphic Bonds

In light, our spirits soar,
Together, we embrace the grace.
In whispers soft as morning dew,
Our hearts find their holy place.

Through trials fierce and shadows deep,
A bond unbroken, pure and bright.
With every prayer, our souls will keep,
A lantern in the darkest night.

From dawn to dusk, in sacred trust,
We walk together hand in hand.
In love, like gold, we turn to dust,
Yet rise anew, as heaven planned.

In unity, the heavens sing,
A chorus woven with each breath.
In faith, we find the joy we bring,
United even beyond death.

In every heartbeat, whispers flow,
Seraphic bonds, forever tied.
Let love's eternal river grow,
In grace, our hearts shall abide.

The Poetry of Togetherness

In every gaze, a story unfolds,
A tapestry of lives entwined.
In laughter shared and warmth, it molds,
A sacred bond that's redefined.

Like sunlight breaking through the rain,
Our hearts align with gentle grace.
In unity, we share the pain,
And in our joy, the world we face.

Through trials faced, with courage bold,
Together, we shall rise above.
In whispers soft, our dreams retold,
Each moment carved in truth and love.

With every prayer, we find our way,
Our voices lift, a sacred sound.
In harmony, we seize the day,
In faith, our spirits unbound.

Together we create a light,
A beacon shining bright and true.
In every step, a pure delight,
The poetry of me and you.

Celestial Symphony

In twilight's hush, the stars align,
Each note a whisper, sweet and pure.
In rhythm soft, our souls entwine,
    A dance of grace we all endure.

The heavens echo with our song,
In harmony, the worlds embrace.
A symphony where we belong,
In love, we find our rightful place.

With every heartbeat, chords resound,
    Together, we compose our fate.
In every moment, joy is found,
    A sacred trust we cultivate.

In light's embrace, time gently sways,
    Each melody a glimpse divine.
In faith, we weave through all our days,
    A celestial bond, forever mine.

Through trials faced, our spirits rise,
A timeless harmony we create.
In the silence, we see the skies,
With love, our hearts resonate.

Divine Murmurs

In whispers soft, the heavens speak,
In every breath, divinity.
With open hearts, we dare to seek,
A sacred realm, eternity.

In moments shared, we feel the light,
A dance of souls, a gentle grace.
Through shadows cast, we find our sight,
In love, we discover our place.

With every prayer that we release,
The sacred flow of spirit moves.
In silence, we find perfect peace,
Where joy and faith forever proves.

In unity, our voices rise,
A chorus blessed by heaven's hand.
Divine murmurs in the skies,
In grace, we walk across this land.

Together, we embrace the dawn,
In every heartbeat, truth revealed.
In love's embrace, we carry on,
Divine murmurs, forever sealed.

Revered Journeys of the Heart

In the quiet hush of morning light,
We walk together, hearts in flight.
With faith as our guide, so strong and true,
Each step we take is born anew.

Through valleys deep and mountains high,
We seek the path that leads us nigh.
With whispers soft from skies above,
Our journey speaks of sacred love.

The trials faced, yet hand in hand,
In unity, we make our stand.
The heart's true quest, a noble chart,
In every beat, we find the art.

With every tear, joy's laughter blooms,
In sacred spaces, hope resumes.
We rise with grace, through thick and thin,
On journeys woven, our souls begin.

And as the sun sets gold and bright,
We honor love, our guiding light.
In this revered path, we find our part,
Together bound in the heart's own chart.

Celestial Echoes of Mutual Affection

In the stillness of the starry night,
Hearts entwined, we feel the light.
With whispers sweet from spirits near,
Our bond is blessed, eternally clear.

Through cosmic waves and endless skies,
Love's gentle pull, the heart's prize.
Like constellations, shining bright,
Each moment shared ignites the night.

In sacred silence, our souls align,
With every heartbeat, love's design.
Celestial echoes, soft and pure,
In mutual affection, we endure.

Each glance a promise, every sigh,
In unity's grace, we learn to fly.
Through trials weathered, hand in hand,
In the vast expanse, together we stand.

As dawn approaches, painted hues,
We honor the path we've come to choose.
In celestial echoes, love's sweet song,
We find our place where we belong.

The Bloom of Unified Souls

In gardens lush, where flowers grow,
United souls begin to show.
With petals bright, they dance and sway,
In gentle breezes, love's bouquet.

Each moment shared, a fragrant bliss,
In every hug, a sacred kiss.
Through seasons change, we nurture life,
In bloom together, free from strife.

Roots intertwined beneath the earth,
We celebrate our sacred birth.
Through trials faced and joys anew,
In every color, love shines through.

As raindrops fall, we rise anew,
In unison, our hearts pursue.
With sunlit skies and moonlit nights,
In love's embrace, we find our heights.

And when the blossoms softly fade,
Our souls remain, a sweet cascade.
In the bloom of unified hearts,
We honor life, where love imparts.

The Harmonious Dawn

As morning breaks with hues of gold,
The day unfolds, the story told.
In harmony, our spirits rise,
A gentle breeze, the dawn's surprise.

Each ray of sunlight warms the soul,
In love's embrace, we feel whole.
Together, hand in hand we stand,
In faith and trust, united as planned.

With every heartbeat, hope restores,
In sacred moments, love explores.
The dawn ignites our shared desire,
In unity, we lift each other higher.

Through trials faced and dreams pursued,
In every challenge, love's renewed.
The harmonious dawn reveals the way,
As shadows fade and night gives way.

With grateful hearts, we welcome light,
In every step, the future bright.
Together bound, our journey spun,
In the harmonious dawn, we've won.

The Promise of Tomorrow

In the dawn, a whisper sings,
Hope unfolds on gentle wings.
Faith in shadows, light will grow,
Tomorrow brings what we bestow.

Every tear, a seed we sow,
In the garden, love will glow.
Through the trials, hand in hand,
A brighter day, we will withstand.

The sky ablaze with colors bright,
Promises etched in morning light.
With each breath, a vow we take,
In sacred trust, our hearts awake.

Trust the journey, follow grace,
In every moment, seek His face.
With gentle hearts, we lift our prayer,
The promise of tomorrow, we will share.

Sacred Vows in Bloom

Underneath the arching trees,
Whispers dance upon the breeze.
In this moment, love's embrace,
Sacred vows our hearts will trace.

Petals fall with every pledge,
Binding souls on timeless edge.
Hand in hand and eyes aligned,
In this bond, our fates entwined.

Every heartbeat, soft and true,
Echoes of vows in morning dew.
In the silence, our spirits weave,
A tapestry we believe.

As the sun begins to rise,
We are one beneath the skies.
In the garden, dreams unfold,
A testament in petals bold.

Everlasting Flame

In the night, a candle glows,
Its gentle warmth, our spirit knows.
Through the shadows, bright it stands,
An everlasting flame in hands.

Each flicker tells a story clear,
Of love enduring, free from fear.
In the stillness, hearts ignite,
The promise shines with purest light.

Through the storms, our light remains,
Uplifting dreams amidst the strains.
In each moment, hope reclaims,
The power of our sacred flames.

Let the vision never fade,
In devotion, unafraid.
As time flows, our spirits soar,
In the light, forevermore.

Serenity's First Glimpse

In the whisper of the morn,
New beginnings gently born.
With our hearts, we seek the still,
Finding peace within the will.

Clouds disperse, the sunlight beams,
Awakening our deepest dreams.
In the silence, soft and clear,
Serenity draws ever near.

Through the chaos, calm we seek,
In the quiet, love is meek.
With each breath, a chance to grow,
In tranquility, our spirits flow.

Hold the moment, cherish grace,
In the quiet, find our place.
For in stillness, truth prevails,
Serenity on whispered trails.

Luminous Bonds of Eternity

In the stillness of dawn's embrace,
Hearts intertwine, a sacred space.
Whispers dance on the breeze of prayer,
Promises echo in devotion's care.

Guided by light, the spirits soar,
Uniting in love forevermore.
Through trials faced, we stand as one,
Bound by faith till life is done.

The stars above, a celestial sign,
Our lives entwined, in love divine.
In every moment, a glimpse of grace,
Eternity's light, in our shared place.

Together we walk, hand in hand,
Facing the storms, we take our stand.
With every heartbeat, we draw near,
In luminous bonds, we lose our fear.

As the sun sets, our spirits rise,
In sacred realms, beyond the skies.
For love transcends, a timeless thread,
In the eternal light, we are forever led.

The Morning of Merged Souls

Awakening with the dawn's soft glow,
Two souls united, a sacred flow.
With hearts aligned in prayerful grace,
We journey together in this holy space.

The morning light, a canvas so bright,
Painting our path in divine light.
In silence shared, our spirits sing,
An offering of love, our souls' spring.

Every heartbeat a sacred vow,
In the sanctum of now, we humbly bow.
With whispers soft, we share our dreams,
In love's embrace, the world redeems.

Hand in hand, through trials we tread,
In every tear, our hearts are fed.
Trusting the journey, the path we choose,
With faith as our guide, we'll never lose.

As the sun ascends, we stand as one,
Two souls awakened, the day begun.
With love everlasting, forever bright,
In the morning's warmth, we find our light.

Glorified Hues of Affection

Brushstrokes of love paint the canvas of time,
In radiant hues, we begin to climb.
Each color a promise, each shade a kiss,
In the gallery of hearts, we find our bliss.

Among the flowers, in gardens we roam,
Finding in laughter, our true home.
Underneath the azure, with arms open wide,
In glorified moments, we take pride.

With every glance, a fervent spark,
Illuminating the shadows, lighting the dark.
Together as one, our spirits entwine,
In the tapestry woven, your heart is mine.

The sky blushes deeply, as the sun begins to set,
A symphony of colors we shan't forget.
In the echoes of love, our souls will sway,
In glorified hues, we'll find our way.

Years may pass, and seasons may shift,
Yet love's pure light is the greatest gift.
Forever cherished, this bond we hold,
In every heartbeat, our story told.

Revelation of the Heart's Sanctuary

Within the silence, truth is unveiled,
A sanctuary where love has prevailed.
Echoes of kindness fill the air,
In the heart's embrace, we find our prayer.

Waves of compassion, the soul's own tide,
In revelation, we walk side by side.
Each moment a treasure, each touch a grace,
In the warmth of your gaze, I find my place.

The whispers of angels guide our path,
In every challenge, we find our wrath.
United in faith, we rise and fall,
For the heart's sanctuary welcomes all.

With every trial, we come to see,
The strength of love, the power to be.
In the stillness, the truth ignites,
In revelation's glow, we find our light.

As the stars bear witness to our vow,
In the heart's sanctuary, we live in the now.
Through love's deep waters, we boldly swim,
In the sacred depths, forever, we brim.

The Sacred Sunlit Path

Upon the earth where shadows fade,
The light descends, a warm cascade.
Each step I take, in faith I tread,
The promises of grace ahead.

In whispers soft, the morning sings,
A symphony, of holy things.
With every breath, a prayer I weave,
In nature's arms, I do believe.

The trees stand tall, in silent praise,
As sunlight dances through the rays.
The path unfolds, a blessed way,
Illuminating night to day.

With open heart, I seek to find,
The sacred truths that heal the mind.
A journey shared with every soul,
In unity, we all are whole.

So let me walk this sunlit track,
With love and faith, I will not lack.
For every step brings closer light,
On sacred paths, in spirit's flight.

Adoration in the First Light

Awake anew, the dawn appears,
With golden hues that calm our fears.
The world is bright, each heart, a song,
In first light's glow, we all belong.

With lifted hands, we greet the sky,
In gratitude, our spirits fly.
The morning's grace, a sweet embrace,
In stillness found, our rightful place.

The birds proclaim a Heaven's call,
In unity, we rise, not fall.
Each moment counts, a precious gift,
In first light's warmth, our souls uplift.

The earth awakens, life anew,
With vibrant colors, pure and true.
In silent wonder, nature speaks,
As peace descends on worn-out peaks.

In adoration, hearts beat strong,
Together, we shall sing our song.
For every dawn, a chance to see,
The love that binds you, and me.

Transcendent Ties

In realms beyond what eyes can view,
Transcendent ties, we feel them true.
A bond unseen, yet deeply felt,
With every soul, affection dwelt.

Through trials faced and joys we share,
In unison, we breathe the air.
From heart to heart, the river flows,
A sacred dance, as love bestows.

The stars above, they light our way,
Reminding us, we're not astray.
In every whisper of the breeze,
We find the strength to bend our knees.

With spirit free, our paths entwined,
In every hug, a heart aligned.
Through love's embrace, we understand,
The universe holds every hand.

So let us cherish, nurture, grow,
These ties that flourish, ever flow.
In unity, our voices rise,
To celebrate the sacred skies.

Hallowed Petals of Passion

In gardens lush, where blossoms bloom,
Hallowed petals chase away gloom.
Each color bright, a tale unfolds,
Of love, of faith, of courage bold.

With fragrant dreams that fill the air,
A symbol sweet, of ardent care.
As petals fall, they whisper low,
The secrets of the heart, we sow.

Through seasons bright, our hearts do dance,
In passion's light, we take a chance.
For love transcends, it never wanes,
In every petal, joy remains.

The beauty lies in tender grace,
As life unfolds, we find our place.
With every breath, our spirits soar,
In hallowed love, forevermore.

Embrace the blooms, both wild and free,
In nature's garden, we shall be.
For passion's fire forever glows,
In hallowed petals, love bestows.

Cherished Visions of Tomorrow

In the dawn's gentle light we see,
Promises woven, a tapestry.
Faith blooms in the hearts that dare,
To dream of a world, pure and fair.

Guided by whispers from above,
Echoes of hope, the song of love.
Each step we take, a sacred trust,
Building our dreams from ashes and dust.

Together we rise, with spirits aligned,
In unity, our souls intertwined.
Cherished visions ignite the night,
Leading us forward to boundless light.

Eyes on horizons, we brave the storms,
For with strength in faith, new life forms.
In every heartbeat, a purpose strong,
In cherished visions, we all belong.

Angels of Affection

Angels above, with wings spread wide,
Whispering comfort, a loving guide.
In shadows deep, they shine so bright,
Guarding our spirits, day and night.

Softly they carry our sorrows away,
Transforming the night into golden day.
With gentle touches, their love unfolds,
In hearts so weary, their warmth consoles.

In every prayer, their presence known,
In silent moments, we're never alone.
When tears fall down like rain from the sky,
Angels of affection, always nearby.

A chorus of joy, they sing near,
Filling our souls with hope and cheer.
In love's sweet embrace, we find our way,
Angels of affection, forever stay.

A Canvas of Celestial Love

In the quiet dawn of a brand-new day,
A canvas unfolds where love finds its way.
Brushstrokes of light, in hues of the soul,
Painting the world, making us whole.

With each drop of rain and glow of the sun,
Nature rejoices, our spirits as one.
Boundless love flows in rivers of grace,
A canvas adorned with the softest embrace.

Stars in the night, like diamonds that gleam,
Whisper the secrets of a Divine dream.
In every heartbeat, in soft, tender sighs,
A tapestry woven, where love never dies.

With colors vibrant, in unity we stand,
Creating a masterpiece, hand in hand.
In the gallery of life, let love be our art,
A canvas of celestial love in every heart.

Embracing the Divine Spirit

In the stillness of night, we gather as one,
Embracing the Divine, our souls weigh a ton.
With open hearts and lifted gaze,
We seek the light that forever stays.

In whispered prayers, our spirits unite,
In moments of silence, we find pure light.
Each breath a blessing, each thought a song,
Embracing the Divine, where we all belong.

The wind carries whispers from realms up above,
Reminding us gently of endless love.
In movement and stillness, in laughter and tears,
The Divine Spirit guides us through our fears.

With arms wide open, let faith lead the way,
In the heart's deep chamber, let us forever stay.
Embracing the Divine, we dance in the grace,
Finding our home in love's warm embrace.

Radiance of the Soul

In the stillness of the night,
The heart begins to rise.
Flickers of divine light,
Guiding us to the skies.

Each breath a holy prayer,
Love surrounds us all.
Lifted by silent care,
In grace we stand tall.

A spark within ignites,
Illuminating the way.
Together, we take flight,
Chasing the dawn's ray.

From darkness, we emerge,
United in the light.
With faith, we gently surge,
Embraced by pure delight.

With every soul's embrace,
We find our truest home.
In this sacred space,
No need for us to roam.

The Covenant of Affection

Beneath the sky so wide,
Hearts intertwine as one.
In love, we safely bide,
While storms of life are spun.

Each moment shared in grace,
A promise carved in stone.
In every warm embrace,
The seeds of hope are sown.

Through trials we shall stand,
Together, hand in hand.
Bound by a sacred strand,
As faith is our command.

In laughter and in tears,
The spirit finds its voice.
Through all our fleeting years,
In love, we shall rejoice.

So let us walk this path,
With joy that brightly glows.
For in compassion's wrath,
The garden of love grows.

Under Heaven's Gaze

In the quiet of the morn,
A whisper fills the air.
With each new day reborn,
We find our souls laid bare.

As stars begin to fade,
The sun paints skies anew.
In shadows, dreams are made,
Guided by purest view.

With faith as our sweet guide,
We walk the sacred ground.
In love we shall abide,
In peace, our hearts are found.

The heavens shed their grace,
As we cast fears aside.
In this enchanted space,
Hearts lift, no need to hide.

Forever under gaze,
Of love that never sleeps.
In truth, our spirits blaze,
And joy within us leaps.

Whispered Devotion

In the stillness of prayer,
Whispers dance on the breeze.
Each thought a sacred layer,
Bringing hearts to their knees.

With every moment shared,
A gentle truth unfolds.
In silence, we are dared,
To trust what love upholds.

Through trials, we find strength,
United in humble grace.
In devotion's sweet length,
There lies a warm embrace.

As dawn breaks on our dreams,
Hope shines like morning dew.
In love's divine extremes,
Our spirits are made new.

With each whispered refrain,
A promise softly sewn.
In the heart's quiet reign,
We find we're never alone.

Promise of the Blessed

In silence we gather, hearts aglow,
With whispered prayers, our spirits grow.
For every tear, a blessing flows,
A promise of peace in love's gentle throes.

Through trials faced, we find our way,
In faith united, come what may.
The light above, it guides our hearts,
A sacred bond that never departs.

In every dawn, new hope is born,
With open arms, we greet the morn.
Together we stand, hands intertwined,
In the promise made, our souls aligned.

With joy we lift our voices high,
In unity, we reach the sky.
The blessings poured, we shall embrace,
In the loving arms of boundless grace.

Reverence of Two Souls

In the quiet night, a prayer is said,
Two souls entwined, by love they're led.
With every heartbeat, the world fades away,
In reverence found, they choose to stay.

Through sacred vows, their spirits soar,
Each whispered promise, a forever door.
In shared devotedness, they find their light,
Two souls as one, in love's pure might.

In the dance of life, they find their grace,
Every challenge met, every embrace.
With faith as their anchor, they aim for the stars,
A bond unbroken, no matter the scars.

The path may be winding, the storms may roar,
Yet side by side, they'll always explore.
With reverence deep, they nurture and grow,
Two souls together, in love's bright glow.

Awakening Hearts

In the still of dawn, hearts begin to rise,
With gentle whispers, beneath the skies.
A call to awaken, to shed the night,
In every breath, there's new found light.

Through valleys of doubt, we seek the sun,
In every moment, we're becoming one.
With hands held firm, we brave each tide,
In opening hearts, there's nothing to hide.

The journey ahead, it unfolds anew,
With faith as our compass, steady and true.
Each step that we take, in grace we trust,
Awakening hearts, in love we must.

In laughter and tears, we dance through the day,
With every heartbeat, we find our way.
Together we rise, with spirits aligned,
Awakening hearts, divinely entwined.

The Sacred Embrace

In the stillness of night, we gather close,
A sacred embrace, what matters most.
With whispered blessings, we find our peace,
In love's pure cradle, all troubles cease.

With arms open wide, we welcome the grace,
Two hearts as one, in a sacred place.
Through trials and joys, together we roam,
In each other's eyes, we find our home.

In the warmth of love, a refuge we make,
In the sacred embrace, no hearts will break.
For every moment shared is a gift divine,
In the light of love, our souls intertwine.

With faith as our anchor, we weather the storm,
In the sacred embrace, we'll be safe and warm.
Together we stand, in shadows or light,
In love's pure embrace, everything feels right.

Spirit's Tender Touch

In the hush of dawn's embrace,
The Spirit whispers soft and low,
Gentle hands that heal the heart,
With love's caress, we come to know.

Beneath the blooming sacred trees,
Where sunlight dances on the stream,
We find the peace our souls have sought,
Awash in love, a holy dream.

Through trials deep and shadows long,
The Comforter's sweet voice remains,
He lifts the weary, mends the soul,
With strength that never fades or wanes.

In quiet moments, trust unfolds,
As faith ignites the path we tread,
With every step, His grace abounds,
In every tear and word unsaid.

Together, in His presence near,
We rise as one in sacred space,
The Spirit's touch, a balm divine,
In love, we find eternal grace.

Rejoicing in His Light

Awake, O heart, to morning's glow,
The light of Him who shines above,
In every beam, His mercy flows,
A boundless sea of endless love.

We gather 'round in joy and song,
With hearts aglow in gratitude,
For every blessing, great and small,
In His embrace, we are renewed.

Through valleys low and mountains high,
His guidance leads our faithful way,
With every step, we walk by faith,
In His light, we find our stay.

The stars that glimmer in the night,
Whisper tales of His great might,
In stillness, we feel His embrace,
Rejoicing in His holy light.

Let every heart lift songs of praise,
To the Creator, kind and wise,
In unity, our voices rise,
Celebrating love that never dies.

Eternal Threads of Union

In tapestry of life entwined,
Our hearts unite, a sacred bond,
With golden threads of faith and hope,
Together, we are ever fond.

Each soul a note in harmony,
A melody of grace and peace,
With every breath, our spirits soar,
In love's embrace, we find release.

Through trials faced, we stand as one,
In darkness, shine our inner light,
With hands held firm, we trust the path,
Guided by love, our hearts ignite.

The promise of forever lingers,
In every laugh, in every tear,
A sacred bond that time can't sever,
In Christ, we find our purpose here.

So let us weave, with threads of love,
A union strong, both bright and bold,
Together, we shall climb the heights,
In God's embrace, our hearts unfold.

Guideposts of Affection

In life's journey, love's soft hands,
Guide our steps through joy and pain,
With every sign, His heart extends,
In tenderness, we find our gain.

Moments shared, a blessed grace,
In laughter's light and sorrow's song,
Through hills and valleys, His love abides,
With each embrace, we all belong.

His guiding voice, a steady beam,
That leads us through the night so cold,
With faith, we walk, a sacred dream,
In warmth of hearts, our lives unfold.

Through trials faced, we grow in strength,
With open hearts and spirits free,
In every challenge, love prevails,
To bind us in unity.

Let us cherish each precious soul,
In every moment, love's sweet call,
For in His arms, we find our home,
Guideposts of affection, one and all.

The Dawn Meets the Heart

In morning light, spirits awake,
The dawn whispers grace, no hearts shall break.
A new day blooms, hope's gentle sigh,
As shadows flee beneath the sky.

Sunrise paints the world anew,
In every face, a love so true.
With open arms, we greet the morn,
To rise and dance, our souls reborn.

In quiet moments, prayers ascend,
In unity we seek to mend.
The soul's soft glow, a guiding star,
Together, we've come, no dream too far.

As sunlight breaks the chains of night,
We walk as one towards the light.
With faith as our anchor, we share the way,
Hand in hand, in love we'll stay.

Firmer Foundations at Sunrise

Bright rays of gold melt the night away,
Each dawn, a chance, a new prayer to say.
With solid ground, our hearts align,
In faith we stand, through storms we shine.

Upon the rocks of kindness laid,
Our dreams take root, in love displayed.
Through trials faced, we build our walls,
In every echo, the Spirit calls.

The sunlit path, our purpose clear,
In every heart, we hold what's dear.
With hands united, we seek His grace,
Our journey marked by His embrace.

Awake, awake! For light does break,
A chorus of hope, for His name's sake.
Firmer foundations, built on trust,
Together we rise, as we must.

The Ascendance of Togetherness

In unity's song, we rise each day,
With strength in numbers, we find our way.
Together, hearts beating as one,
In grace we flourish, though battles be won.

As morning's glow floods the earth,
New beginnings echo our worth.
With open hearts, we share the load,
On this journey, love is the road.

Through trials faced in shared embrace,
We lift each other, finding our place.
The bonds we forge reflect His light,
In every moment, His love ignites.

As the sun reaches high in the sky,
Our spirits soar, we learn to fly.
In togetherness, we find our song,
In every heartbeat, we all belong.

Witnesses to each Sacred Sunrise

Each dawn we gather, hearts entwined,
To witness the promise of love defined.
With every sunrise, a blessing flows,
In radiant beams, the glory shows.

Hands uplifted, we honor the day,
With grateful hearts, we learn to pray.
In silence deep, we hear the call,
As sacred whispers blanket us all.

From shadows cast, we find our way,
In the light of truth, we shall not sway.
In unity's watch, we fulfill His plan,
Together we rise, as brothers and man.

Each moment cherished, a glimpse divine,
In the dance of light, we're bound to shine.
As witnesses to every dawn we see,
In faith and love, we shall forever be.

The Faithful Union

In the garden of love, we stand,
With arms embraced, hand in hand.
Together we rise, hearts afire,
In this sacred bond, we never tire.

Through trials and storms, we remain,
Guided by faith, overcoming pain.
United we shine, through darkest night,
A beacon of hope, a cherished light.

In prayer we gather, voices raised,
In humble submission, our hearts ablaze.
Each whispered word, a sacred song,
In this faithful union, we belong.

With gratitude, we bless the day,
In every step, we find our way.
Bound by spirit, forever true,
In the Lord's embrace, we start anew.

Together we journey, hearts entwined,
In the light of love, our souls aligned.
For in His grace, we find our cheer,
In the faithful union, we persevere.

Hymn of Rebirth

Awake, arise, a new dawn breaks,
In the silence, a soft voice wakes.
From ashes born, we shall ascend,
In the light of hope, our spirits mend.

With every heartbeat, life ignites,
In the distance, a vision bright.
The past released, like autumn's leaves,
In this hymn of rebirth, our heart believes.

With every tear, a river flows,
In trials faced, the spirit grows.
From shadows creeping, we emerge whole,
In the embrace of love, we find our soul.

In gratitude, we lift our song,
To the Creator, where we belong.
With faith renewed, we journey forth,
In every step, the promise of worth.

With each sunrise, we rise anew,
A testament of grace shining through.
In harmony, we join the throng,
In this hymn of rebirth, we grow strong.

In the Light of Grace

In the quiet dawn, His love appears,
Washing away all doubts and fears.
In every shadow, His presence shines,
An anchor of peace, where hope entwines.

In the stillness, we hear His call,
Lifting our spirits, guiding us all.
Each gentle whisper, a loving trace,
Leading us onward, in the light of grace.

Through valleys deep and mountains high,
Our souls uplifted, we learn to fly.
In trials faced, we find our place,
Embraced forever, in the light of grace.

With hearts aglow, we share His word,
Through every action, our voices heard.
In community strong, we share our space,
Transforming the world, in the light of grace.

In each moment, His love surrounds,
With every heartbeat, His presence resounds.
Together we walk, in a holy embrace,
Finding our purpose, in the light of grace.

Cherished among the Stars

In the night sky, our dreams take flight,
We find our path, bathed in light.
Each star a promise, each spark a sigh,
In the arms of the cosmos, we learn to fly.

Embraced by love, we find our place,
A tapestry woven in divine grace.
In every heartbeat, a pulse of truth,
Cherished among the stars, we find our youth.

With every glance, we see His face,
In the vast expanse of sacred space.
Together we rise, with hearts unscarred,
In this journey of faith, forever starred.

In the rhythm of life, our spirits sing,
In harmony blessed, we take to wing.
With open hearts, we boldly trust,
Cherished among the stars, in faith we must.

Under the heavens, united in prayer,
In every moment, we feel Him there.
With love as our guide, we'll go far,
Forever cherished, among the stars.

A New Era of Blessings

In shadows past, we sought the light,
With hope renewed, our spirits bright.
The dawn of grace, a sacred start,
In every soul, a kindred heart.

Through trials faced, we stand as one,
Embracing love, our battles won.
With hands uplifted, prayers we raise,
In unity, we sing His praise.

A tapestry of lives interwoven,
In faith and trust, our path is chosen.
With every step, the blessings flow,
A new beginning we shall sow.

In whispered winds, His voice is clear,
Inviting us to draw near.
In every tear, a lesson learned,
For in His light, our hearts are turned.

So let us walk in love and grace,
And find our strength in His embrace.
Each day a gift, a chance to share,
In kindness met, our burdens bare.

Divine Touch at Dawn

As dawn breaks forth with gentle sighs,
The world awakes, and hope replies.
In every ray, a promise shines,
A divine touch, our hearts align.

With every breath, a prayer we raise,
In stillness found, we seek His ways.
The morning whispers soft and sweet,
In nature's choir, our souls repeat.

Through trials faced, the night we've known,
God's hands support us, never alone.
In every dawn, a chance to grow,
With faith as deep as rivers flow.

The beauty found in every hue,
Reminds us all of love so true.
Each moment blessed, a gift divine,
In gratitude, our lives entwine.

So let us rise with hearts aglow,
Embracing light, our spirits flow.
In each new dawn, we trust and see,
The divine touch that sets us free.

The Call of Kindred Souls

In quiet moments, whispers roam,
A tender call, guiding us home.
With hands outstretched, we seek to find,
The loving bonds that tie mankind.

Through trials faced, we learn to share,
Together walking, light as air.
In each embrace, a blessing warm,
In joy and pain, we bear each storm.

In sacred circles, hearts unite,
Together shining, pure as light.
With every voice, a symphony,
That echoes through eternity.

As kindred souls, we lift each other,
In love's embrace, we find our brother.
In every tear, in laughter's song,
We weave a tale where all belong.

So heed the call, let spirits soar,
In faith and trust, forevermore.
For in this bond, our hearts shall rest,
In love divine, we are truly blessed.

Elysium in the Morning

In morning light, a promise wakes,
Elysium's grace, our hearts it takes.
A sacred breath, a still embrace,
In every dawn, we seek His face.

With whispered prayers, we rise anew,
With faith renewed, our dreams pursue.
In nature's song, His love resounds,
In every heart, His truth abounds.

Through valleys deep, where shadows lay,
He guides us forth, our fears allay.
With hope aglow, we journey on,
Through trials faced, we are reborn.

In every step, a dance of grace,
Together we shall find our place.
With spirits high, we lift our gaze,
In Elysium, we give Him praise.

So let our hearts in unity beat,
In love we find, our lives complete.
For every morn, a gift we hold,
A story blessed, forever told.

Frequencies of Faithful Affection

In the quiet of prayer, hearts align,
Whispers of love, pure and divine.
Hands uplifted towards the sky,
Echoes of faith, never to die.

Each soul a note in the sacred choir,
Bound by the truth, a heavenly fire.
In moments of doubt, love's light guides,
Together we stand, where hope abides.

Through trials and storms, our spirits sing,
Faithful affection, a wondrous thing.
In every challenge, together we find,
The strength of devotion, forever combined.

We walk a path, hand in hand,
United in grace, we make our stand.
Every heartbeat, a prayer we share,
In the frequencies of love, we are aware.

The Beatitude of Union

In valleys low, and mountains high,
The bond of love will never die.
Each gentle soul, a light so bright,
Together we rise, into the night.

The blessing of union, pure and sweet,
In every heartbeat, our fates meet.
A tapestry woven, divine in grace,
In the garden of life, we find our place.

With every breath, we seek the truth,
In laughter and tears, we find our youth.
Through trials faced, and joys shared wide,
The beatitude of love will be our guide.

In harmony's promise, we shall dwell,
Each moment a story, in love we tell.
Bound by the spirit, forever we'll shine,
Together, unified, the sacred design.

The Ethereal Garden of Togetherness

In an ethereal garden, where flowers bloom,
Love intertwines, dispelling the gloom.
Every petal a prayer, soft and light,
Together we flourish, in day and night.

In the breeze of grace, we sway and dance,
Sharing the beauty of love's sweet chance.
Each moment a treasure, shared from the heart,
In the garden of togetherness, never apart.

With roots intertwined, we grow as one,
Beneath the vast sky, kissed by the sun.
Every memory cherished, every laugh a song,
In this sacred haven, where we belong.

Through seasons of change, our love will stay,
In the ethereal garden, we'll find our way.
Hand in hand, we'll tread this ground,
In the whispers of nature, love's voice is found.

Morning Light upon Our Spirits

Awake to the dawn, as the light breaks through,
A promise of hope in the sky's soft hue.
Each ray a blessing, each breath a gift,
In morning's embrace, our spirits lift.

The warmth of the sun, a gentle caress,
Invites us to rise, in love we confess.
With hearts open wide, we embrace the day,
Guided by faith, in love's sacred way.

From shadows of night, to light so bright,
We walk in grace, in the morning light.
Expressions of love, as soft as a sigh,
With every new dawn, we reach for the sky.

In the stillness of morn, we find our peace,
A moment of prayer that will never cease.
With hands open wide, in gratitude we stand,
In the morning light, we understand.

The Sacred Kiss

In sacred silence, hearts entwine,
A whisper soft as holy wine.
With reverence, we seek your grace,
In every moment, find your face.

Fingers touch like warmest rays,
Illuminating sacred ways.
In stillness, breathe the love we share,
A holy bond beyond compare.

Oh, lead us to your blessed throne,
Where every soul may call you home.
In trust, we lift our hearts to thee,
For in your light, we are set free.

With every glance, a promise made,
In every tear, your love displayed.
Embraced in love, no fear remains,
Our sacred kiss, eternal gains.

In the stillness, hear our prayer,
A longing deep as the ocean's stare.
We journey on, your hand in hand,
Forever bound in love so grand.

Unveiling the Beloved

In shadows deep, your light we seek,
Through veils of doubt, you make us meek.
With open hearts, we call your name,
In every soul, a burning flame.

Unveil the truth in each embrace,
Reveal the depths of boundless grace.
As dawn breaks forth, so love awakes,
In unity, our spirit shakes.

Through trials faced, we find our way,
In whispered prayers, our hopes we lay.
With every step, our faith will grow,
In you, beloved, we deeply know.

The mirror shows, your face is ours,
In every challenge, we find the stars.
Awakened souls, together rise,
Unveiling love beyond the skies.

In sacred moments, we draw near,
In all our joys, you are the cheer.
Through loving grace, we come alive,
With open hearts, we learn to thrive.

The Dance of Light

In rhythmic waves, the spirit sways,
In every heart, a tune that plays.
With hands uplifted, shadows flee,
We dance in light, we dance in thee.

With every step, we feel the grace,
In every turn, your warm embrace.
The music swells, our voices rise,
In sacred dance, we touch the skies.

Oh, luminous one, guide our way,
In joyful hearts, let love hold sway.
The symphony of souls takes flight,
In the eternal, purest light.

As time unfolds, a sacred thread,
In every move, the words unsaid.
Through sacred dance, we find our voice,
In every moment, love's sweet choice.

Together bound, in harmony,
In every breath, we worship thee.
With hearts ablaze, we'll never part,
In this grand dance, you own our heart.

Divine Union

In every heartbeat, love resounds,
In sacred silence, truth abounds.
With arms extended, we draw near,
In divine union, nothing to fear.

Your whispers beckon, we obey,
In tender night and sunlit day.
With souls entwined, we rise as one,
In witness of the holy sun.

Within your essence, we are whole,
In unity, we seek our goal.
As rivers flow, and mountains stand,
We walk together, hand in hand.

Oh, guide our hearts, forever bless,
In gentle peace, our souls caress.
In love's embrace, we find our place,
In divine union, endless grace.

Through trials faced, our strength will show,
In every tear, your love will flow.
With gratitude, we stand as one,
In divine union, love begun.

Cherubs in Love

In skies adorned with gentle light,
Two cherubs dance, hearts taking flight.
With laughter sweet, they weave their song,
In realms above, where love is strong.

They whisper prayers on clouds so high,
Their grace flows down like softest sigh.
In tender dreams, they hold the night,
Each heartbeat echoes pure delight.

With wings that shimmer, they create,
A bond that's woven, a sacred state.
In every glance, a world unfolds,
A story shared, a tale of gold.

They soar through heavens, hand in hand,
In circles spun, their spirits stand.
With every flutter, hearts align,
In love's embrace, the stars they shine.

Forever blessed, they write their fate,
In holy love, they celebrate.
Two cherubs bright, in light they dwell,
Their hearts entwined, a blissful spell.

The Morning of Grace

Awakening dawn, the sun's embrace,
A gift renewed, the morning of grace.
Soft whispers of hope in the gentle air,
Calling the heart to rise, to share.

Each dewdrop glistens, a promise made,
In fields of faith, the shadows fade.
With open hearts, we greet the day,
In love's warm light, we'll find our way.

In sacred silence, we seek the truth,
The warmth of kindness, the joy of youth.
With every footstep on sacred ground,
In gratitude and grace, our voices sound.

The birds take flight, in heaven's choir,
Their melodies lift us ever higher.
In prayers we whisper, our hopes take wing,
In the morning light, our souls will sing.

With every heartbeat, we walk this path,
In love's embrace, we find our math.
Together we wander, forever to chase,
The beauty divine in the morning of grace.

Shepherded Hearts

In valleys deep, where the shadows play,
The shepherd calls, guiding the way.
With gentle hands, he leads the weak,
In love profound, his heart will speak.

Through trials faced, we find our peace,
In trust we blossom, worries cease.
Together as one, through storms we'll roam,
In united hearts, we find our home.

With faith as our staff and hope as our shield,
In every embrace, our strength revealed.
Through meadows green and skies of blue,
The shepherd's heart will guide us true.

In lessons learned and joys imparted,
From every sorrow, we are guarded.
In every prayer, our spirits start,
To rise in love, shepherded hearts.

As stars ignite the darkened night,
In every dream, we see the light.
With grateful souls, we sing our part,
In unison loud, shepherded hearts.

The Garden of Affection

In the garden where the flowers bloom,
Love paints a path, dispelling gloom.
Each petal whispers a sacred prayer,
Encircling souls with tender care.

The sun casts warmth on roots that cling,
In fertile soil, new feelings spring.
With gentle rains, our spirits grow,
In cherished moments, love will flow.

With every blossom, a promise spoken,
In fragrant dreams, no hearts are broken.
Together we cultivate, hand in hand,
In the garden of affection, we'll always stand.

Beneath the trellis, where shadows dance,
We find our solace, a blissful trance.
In laughter shared and tears embraced,
In the garden, love finds its place.

Through seasons change, the love remains,
In blooms of hope, our joy sustains.
In every heart, a seed we sow,
In the garden of affection, forever to grow.

Morning Blessings of Affection

In the dawn's gentle glow, we rise,
Hearts united in prayer and sighs.
With every breath, love's hymn we sing,
To the source of joy, our souls take wing.

Gracious light spills across the land,
Guiding us through His faithful hand.
Each moment shared in holy grace,
Transforms our hearts in warm embrace.

Morning whispers of peace abound,
In His presence, solace is found.
The blessings flow like rivers wide,
With faith as our everlasting guide.

From the heavens, a sacred call,
We gather together, one and all.
In love's embrace, we find our way,
Through every trial, come what may.

Let gratitude rise with the sun,
For every battle already won.
With morning's blessings, we are blessed,
In the arms of love, we find our rest.

Divine Whispers at Sunrise

At sunrise, whispers soft and clear,
Echoes embrace, drawing us near.
In the stillness, a sacred sound,
Promising hope in love profound.

Golden rays paint the waking sky,
In silence, our hearts learn to fly.
Through the warmth of the morning light,
We feel His presence, pure and bright.

With every dawn, a chance to see,
The beauty of our divinity.
Each step forward, a prayer we share,
Elating our spirits, laid bare.

A blessed path illuminated,
In faith and love, we're integrated.
In the depth of the morning's grace,
Our souls find rest in His embrace.

Let us walk in the light bestowed,
With hearts as pure as love's true road.
In divine whispers, we find our worth,
Celebrating life, our sacred birth.

Celestial Bonds Revealed

In the quiet dawn, spirits align,
Celestial bonds, pure and divine.
Heaven's song in the morning breeze,
Whispers of love bring us to our knees.

Each heartbeat echoes a sacred tune,
Under the watchful eye of the moon.
In every smile, a light is found,
In love's embrace, our souls are bound.

Remember the promises made above,
In faith unyielding, wrapped in love.
With every sunrise, a chance to be,
The embodiment of unity.

As the heavens paint the skies anew,
We gather strength from love so true.
In the tapestry of life we weave,
The bonds of heaven help us believe.

May our hearts beat as one in grace,
In unity, we find our place.
Celestial whispers guide our way,
In their light, we shall always stay.

Radiance of Devotion

In the morning's glow, a promise shines,
Radiance of devotion intertwines.
With every prayer, we seek to know,
The strength of faith in love's warm flow.

Life's journey beckons, hand in hand,
With hearts uplifted, we make our stand.
In the stillness, our spirits soar,
In devotion's light, we choose to explore.

The sun rises high, casting shadows away,
Guided by love, we greet the day.
With gratitude, we open wide,
The doors of our hearts, letting love inside.

In every moment, His words resonate,
Filling our souls, absolving our fate.
In the radiance of divine embrace,
We find our purpose, our sacred space.

Let our lives be a beacon bright,
Shining forth with faith and light.
For in devotion's boundless sea,
We discover the essence of being free.

Heartstrings Alight

In the silence of the night,
We gather strength from love's light.
Whispers soft guide our way,
As we seek the truth each day.

Hearts entwined in sacred space,
Finding solace in His grace.
In every tear that we shed,
Hope arises, softly led.

With each prayer, our spirits soar,
A holy bond forevermore.
Radiant faith ignites the flame,
Through our surrender, we exclaim.

Together we walk the divine path,
In unity, we spark His wrath.
Break the chains that hold us near,
In reverence, we cast out fear.

Let heartstrings weave a tapestry,
Of love and light, eternally.
In our souls, His love ignites,
As we dance in gentle light.

The Sacred Circle

Gathered 'round in sacred space,
Reverence flows like a soft embrace.
In the circle, we stand as one,
In the dawn, our spirits run.

With voices raised in unity,
We sing hymns of community.
The earth draws us, roots entwine,
In this holy space, we shine.

Hands held high, we cast our dreams,
In the heart's light, all redeems.
Echoes of love resound the call,
In the circle, we are all.

Moments shared in trust profound,
In this sacred love, we're bound.
Through every trial, stand as allies,
In this circle, our hope flies.

As the sun dips, shadows fall,
We rise together, answering the call.
Bound in heart and spirit's kiss,
In this sacred circle, we find bliss.

A Radiant Communion

In the quietude we connect,
In gratitude, we reflect.
Each breath a sacred offering,
In love's embrace, our souls sing.

Under the stars, hearts unite,
A tapestry of purest light.
In this communion, spirits soar,
Love enfolds us, evermore.

With gentle hands, we share our dreams,
In community, hope redeems.
Through trials faced, we find the grace,
In divine love, we find our place.

Together we weave, life's threads divine,
In rhythm and flow, our hearts align.
Each moment cherished, a gift divine,
A radiant light, forever shine.

As dawn awakens, shadows flee,
In this communion, we are free.
With every heartbeat, love extends,
In radiant unity, our journey blends.

Threads of Eternity

In the loom of life, threads intertwine,
Woven together, your heart with mine.
Through storms we weather, side by side,
In faith unyielding, we take the tide.

As time unfurls its sacred scroll,
Each moment lived, we nourish the soul.
In love's embrace, we find our strength,
Together we journey, across the length.

Our stories blend in the grand design,
In the fabric of grace, we forever shine.
Each thread a memory, precious and true,
In the tapestry of time, we are renewed.

With hope as the needle, stitching our fate,
In every heartbeat, we celebrate.
Through valleys low and mountains high,
In threads of eternity, we learn to fly.

As light shines down, guiding our way,
In unity, we welcome each day.
With every thread, our legacy stays,
In love's tapestry, forever raises.

Awakening Hearts

In silence, the spirit stirs anew,
With whispers of love, gentle and true.
Awake, O hearts, to the light of grace,
Let mercy and hope find their rightful place.

The dawn breaks soft on a world so wide,
With faith as our compass, we walk beside.
Each step emboldened, our path will shine,
In unity we rise, your heart is mine.

Divine light shines on each weary soul,
Restoring the broken, making us whole.
Hearts once heavy now dancing free,
In love's great embrace, we find our plea.

Awakening dreams within the night,
Transforming shadows into pure light.
In every heartbeat, a sacred song,
Together we find where we belong.

So let us gather, hand in hand,
Creating a tapestry, a sacred land.
With each pulse of love, let us begin,
Awakening hearts, together we win.

The Divine Embrace

In the quiet moments where stillness lays,
The Divine whispers softly in tender ways.
With arms wide open, love does extend,
In the heart's pure longing, we find a friend.

Through trials and triumphs, we wander bold,
In tales of the faithful, our stories unfold.
Each tear that falls, a prayer in disguise,
In the Divine's embrace, our hope never dies.

The warmth of the sun, a reminder to grace,
Inviting the weary to seek a safe place.
With every heartbeat, a promise we weave,
That trust in the Lord will never deceive.

In shadows we linger, yet light breaks through,
In the depths of our sorrow, love finds its hue.
Let burdens be lifted, be free from the weight,
In the Divine embrace, we commune with fate.

Together we rise on this sacred ground,
In moments of darkness, love's light will be found.
With each breath we take, an anthem we sing,
In the Divine embrace, new life takes wing.

Morning's Sacred Promise

With the dawn breaks a promise, pure and bright,
A canvas of hope kissed by morning light.
Each dewdrop glimmers, a moment divine,
In the heart of creation, love's threads entwine.

With every heartbeat, new lifetimes commence,
In stillness, we gather our thoughts to dispense.
The struggles of yesterday gently subside,
As morning unfolds with the warmth of the tide.

Nature's soft chorus sings praises so sweet,
Welcoming blessings in rhythmic repeat.
With eyes open wide, we embrace what is true,
In morning's embrace, the world feels anew.

With courage ignited, let's step forth with grace,
Woven together, our souls interlace.
For in every sunrise, a chance to renew,
Morning's sacred promise, forever in view.

So rise, O spirits, let joy take its course,
In the arms of the day, let love be our force.
With each breath of morning, let hope take its place,
In morning's sacred promise, we find our grace.

A Blossom Unseen

In the garden of life where shadows lay,
A blossom unseen begins to sway.
With roots deep in prayer, it reaches for light,
Transforming the darkness into dazzling sight.

Though buried in soil, its spirit remains,
Dancing with whispers of gentle refrains.
For even in silence, the soul can perceive,
The heart of creation that dares to believe.

In moments of doubt, when hope seems to fade,
Remember the blossom that courage has made.
For strength lies within, though hidden from view,
In the heart of each being, a spirit so true.

With patience, it grows, unearthing its grace,
As faith becomes sunlight, a warm, sweet embrace.
In the tapestry woven of colors untold,
A blossom unseen reveals stories of old.

So cherish each struggle, each tear and each sigh,
For through every tempest, new blooms will arise.
In the journey of life, let your heart be keen,
To seek out the beauty, the blossom unseen.

The Blessing of Togetherness

In unity we gather, hearts in grace,
Hand in hand, we find our sacred space.
Through trials shared, our spirits soar,
In love's embrace, we open the door.

With whispers soft, our prayers align,
In every moment, your light is mine.
Together we rise, with voices sweet,
In the bond of faith, our lives complete.

Through laughter shared, through tears we shed,
A holy journey, where angels tread.
In joy and sorrow, side by side,
In the blessing of love, we abide.

As stars above, our souls entwine,
In the tapestry of the divine.
With each heartbeat, we nod to fate,
In faith's embrace, we celebrate.

In every sunrise, a promise anew,
A sacred rhythm, just me and you.
Together in spirit, forever we'll thrive,
In the light of togetherness, we arrive.

Celestial Ties

Beneath the heavens, our spirits dance,
In the glow of stars, we find our chance.
Through cosmic rhythms, our souls unite,
In the universe's vast, sacred light.

Each heartbeat echoes, a celestial song,
In the fabric of time, we all belong.
Through the laughter of winds, and the whispers of trees,
In the beauty of nature, we are at ease.

With open arms, we embrace the divine,
The love that connects us, a sacred sign.
In every moment, in every sigh,
In the tapestry woven, we rise up high.

The moonlight guides us, through nights so dark,
In the heart of the stillness, we find our spark.
With faith as our beacon, love lights the way,
In celestial ties, forever we'll stay.

Through boundless skies, our dreams take flight,
In the glow of the dawn, we bask in the light.
Together we wander, sojourning souls,
In this cosmic embrace, we are made whole.

Adoration's Gentle Rise

In morning light, our spirits sing,
With hearts awakened, joy we bring.
In humble reverence, we lift our gaze,
To the wonders of love, we offer praise.

With every step, we seek the divine,
In the simple moments, a sacred sign.
Through trials faced, through mountains climbed,
In adoration's rise, we are aligned.

In quiet whispers, our souls convene,
In the dance of grace, an unseen sheen.
With open hearts, we share our dreams,
In love's embrace, the world redeems.

Through every shadow, a light is cast,
In faith's journey, the die is cast.
With gratitude blooming, we stand so tall,
In the rise of love, we answer the call.

In the heartbeat of prayer, we find our way,
With every moment, love leads the sway.
In adoration's gentle rise, we find,
A path of beauty, forever entwined.

Transcendent Connections

In the spirit of love, we find our bond,
In the heart of the universe, we respond.
With every heartbeat, with every prayer,
Transcendent connections, we gladly share.

Through mountains high and valleys low,
In the sacred journeys, our spirits flow.
With compassion's touch, we bridge the divide,
In the light of kindness, we turn the tide.

In moments of silence, our souls arise,
In the depths of stillness, wisdom lies.
With open hearts, we dare to trust,
In transcendent love, we find what's just.

As rivers converge, we learn to flow,
In every connection, love's seeds we sow.
With hope as our anchor, we rise anew,
In the bond of connection, we find what's true.

Through the fabric of life, we weave our threads,
In the embrace of sisterhood, where love spreads.
With every smile, with every grace,
Transcendent connections, our hearts embrace.

Heavenly Threads of Connection

In the gentle weft of grace,
We find our souls entwined.
Each whisper of the heart
A testament aligned.

Across the vast expanse,
A tapestry of light,
Anchored by faith's embrace,
We soar into the night.

With every silent prayer,
We weave a stronger bond,
Illuminating shadows,
A love that goes beyond.

In unity we rise,
With hands gently clasped,
In the glow of divinity,
Our spirits are unmasked.

Together we shall walk,
On paths of pure devotion,
Bound by sacred threads,
In eternal motion.

Tender Awakening of the Spirit

Awaken gently, heart,
In the dawn's tender light.
The Spirit whispers soft,
Guiding you toward flight.

With each breath, there's promise,
A love both vast and near,
In harmony we rise,
Transcending doubt and fear.

Morning dew upon the grass,
A sign of blessed rebirth,
In every tiny moment,
We uncover our worth.

Let the silence cradle you,
In stillness, find your way,
With joy, engage the world,
A vibrant hymn of praise.

In unity, we flourish,
As petals greet the sun,
In the garden of the spirit,
We are forever one.

The Illuminated Path of Desire

Desire shines like starlight,
A beacon in the night.
It draws us ever closer,
To realms of pure delight.

With every step we take,
Our hearts blaze bright and clear,
In pursuit of the sacred,
We conquer doubt and fear.

The path may twist and turn,
But faith will light the way,
Each yearning leads us home,
To joys we can't betray.

Embrace the sacred quest,
For love ignites the fire,
In every pulse we feel,
Awakens our desire.

Together we shall journey,
Through valleys deep and wide,
With the light of our longing,
As our eternal guide.

Sacred Vows at Daybreak

As dawn breaks gently forth,
We speak our sacred vows,
Promises etched in time,
In love's eternal bow.

With every softened whisper,
Our hearts take flight anew,
In the canvas of the morn,
We paint a world so true.

Lit by the warmth of hope,
Hand in hand, we embrace,
In the presence of the divine,
We find our sacred place.

Each word a tender blessing,
An echo of the soul,
In the realm of the spirit,
Together we are whole.

As day unfolds before us,
In the light, we remain,
Bound by sacred vows,
In joy and love's domain.

Elysian Embrace

In the garden where angels tread,
Whispers of love softly spread.
Hands reaching through celestial light,
Souls entwined in sacred night.

Dreams adorned with heavenly grace,
Hearts entwined in a warm embrace.
Stars above sing praises bright,
Guiding us through the endless night.

With every prayer, we take flight,
Carried on wings of pure delight.
In unity, our spirits soar,
Finding peace forevermore.

Elysium calls in vocals sweet,
In the stillness, our hearts meet.
In this bond, we shall reside,
Together, forever side by side.

Through trials, we find our way,
In love's embrace, we choose to stay.
With every heartbeat, we transcend,
In the light of love, we mend.

Holy Threads of Connection

Woven closely, souls align,
Threads of faith, a sacred sign.
In the tapestry of light,
Bonded hearts unite in flight.

Voices raised in harmony,
A symphony of purity.
Every whisper, every prayer,
Guides us to the love we share.

Hands united, we stand tall,
Together, we shall never fall.
With grace, we weave our dreams anew,
In the fabric of love so true.

Moments sweet, so divine,
In your strength, I find my shine.
A connection that cannot break,
In every step, our hearts awake.

In holy light, we celebrate,
Bound together, we elevate.
With every breath, we draw near,
In this bond, there's naught to fear.

Light from the Heart's Altar

Upon the altar of the soul,
Love's light reflects, making us whole.
With every beat, our spirits flare,
In this sanctuary, we lay bare.

Illuminated by the sacred flame,
We find solace in His name.
With open hearts, we come alive,
In this light, we shall thrive.

Minds in prayer, spirits aligned,
In silence, our truths entwined.
Each thought a whisper, pure and bright,
Guiding us through the darkest night.

Sacred echoes fill the air,
Boundless love beyond compare.
In every heartbeat, grace pours free,
The altar gives us clarity.

Together we rise, hand in hand,
In this warmth, forever we stand.
With faith as our shining guide,
On this path, we shall abide.

Ethereal Dance of Desire

In twilight's glow, our spirits waltz,
A dance of longing, love's exalt.
Veiled in silence, breaths entwined,
In the depths, our hearts aligned.

Every glance, a spark ignites,
In harmony, we take our flights.
Unseen rhythms pull us near,
In this dance, there's naught to fear.

Whispers soft, like sacred prayers,
In each step, our love declares.
With every twirl, we rise, we fall,
Drawn together, one and all.

Beyond the veil, our spirits twine,
In the twilight, divine design.
Ethereal moves beneath the moon,
In this dance, we're lost in tune.

As shadows lengthen, we remain,
In this moment, free from pain.
The universe in our embrace,
An ethereal, timeless grace.

Blessings in Morning's Glow

As dawn breaks with soft light,
Whispers of grace fill the air.
Heaven's touch in each ray,
Awakening hearts with care.

Birds sing hymns to the morn,
Nature rejoices in praise.
Each moment a golden gift,
Guiding us through our days.

Hands lifted in thankfulness,
Eyes closed, spirits set free.
In the stillness we gather,
Finding strength in unity.

Mountains stand tall and proud,
Echoing the love divine.
Every heartbeat's a prayer,
In this sacred design.

In the warmth of the sun's embrace,
We feel His presence near.
Walking paths of devotion,
Our souls rise high, no fear.

The Awakening of Sacred Souls

In the silence of twilight,
Hearts begin to ignite.
Awakening sacred truths,
Guided by heavenly light.

Each thought is a blessing,
Each prayer a soft song.
Together we rise in hope,
In faith, we become strong.

The stars hold their secrets,
Whispering love from above.
Drawing us closer each night,
In a tapestry of love.

Humble journeys we cherish,
Steps taken hand in hand.
In the dance of our spirits,
Together we will stand.

Through valleys and mountains,
We see the path unfold.
In the warmth of compassion,
Awakening spirits bold.

Journey into the Light of Togetherness

In the distance, faint glimmers,
A call to love we find.
Together we walk forward,
Leaving darkness behind.

With compassion as our guide,
We step on sacred ground.
Sharing laughter and wisdom,
In each other, life's profound.

The road may twist and turn,
Yet unity leads us right.
Hand in hand, hearts entwined,
We journey into the light.

Every voice lifts a prayer,
Echoes of joy abound.
In the warmth of togetherness,
A deeper grace is found.

With each sunset and sunrise,
We cherish what we've known.
In this journey of the spirit,
Love is our cornerstone.

Unity in the Quiet Dawn

As the world awakens slow,
We find peace in the still.
In the quiet of dawn's embrace,
Our spirits learn to fill.

Gathered under the heavens,
Hearts aligned in one beat.
Finding solace in whispers,
Where divinity and life meet.

Nature's breath sings of hope,
Each bloom a sacred sign.
In the morning's soft hymn,
We feel His love, divine.

Through the shadows of existence,
Radiance begins to rise.
With unity in the stillness,
We find grace in the ties.

In the heart of the dawn's light,
We celebrate the day.
In unity, we awaken,
Guided by love, we stay.

Milton Keynes UK
Ingram Content Group UK Ltd.
UKHW031321271124
451618UK00007B/163